Visit
WALES

WALES

NORTH
AMERICA

EUROPE

ASIA

AFRICA

SOUTH
AMERICA

AUSTRALIA

Chris Oxlade and Anita Ganeri

Heinemann
LIBRARY

www.heinemann.co.uk/library

Visit our website to find out more information about **Heinemann Library** books.

To order:

 Phone 44 (0) 1865 888066

 Send a fax to 44 (0) 1865 314091

 Visit the Heinemann Bookshop at www.heinemann.co.uk/library to browse our catalogue and order online.

First published in Great Britain by Heinemann Library, Halley Court, Jordan Hill, Oxford OX2 8EJ, part of Harcourt Education. Heinemann is a registered trademark of Harcourt Education Ltd.

Editorial: Nicole Irving and Georga Godwin
Design: Ron Kamen and StoreyBooks
Picture Research: Catherine Bevan and Ginny Stroud-Lewis
Production: Sévy Ribierre

Originated by Dot Gradations Ltd
Printed and bound in China by South China Printing Company

ISBN 0 431 08270 7
07 06 05 04 03
10 9 8 7 6 5 4 3 2 1

British Library Cataloguing in Publication Data
Oxlade, Chris and Ganeri, Anita
Visit Wales
914.29
A full catalogue record for this book is available from the British Library.

Acknowledgements
The Publishers would like to thank the following for permission to reproduce photographs: Action Plus p. **24**; Collections/Ken Price p. **28**; Corbis pp. **5**, **6**; Food Features p. **13**; John Walmsley p. **22**; Peter Evans pp. **7**, **8**, **10**, **11**, **12**, **18**, **19**, **20**, **21**, **25**, **29**; The Photo Library Wales/Steve Benbow pp. **14**, **23**; The Photolibrary Wales/David Williams p. **9**; The Photolibrary Wales/Kathy De Witt p. **26**; The Photolibrary Wales/Simon Regan p. **16**; Trip/M. Barlow pp. **15**, **27**; Trip/P. Rauter p. **17**.

Cover photograph of Conway Castle in Gwynedd, reproduced with permission of The Photolibrary Wales/Harry Williams.

Every effort has been made to contact copyright holders of any material reproduced in this book. Any omissions will be rectified in subsequent printings if notice is given to the Publishers.

Contents

Any words appearing in bold, **like this**, are explained in the Glossary.

Wales

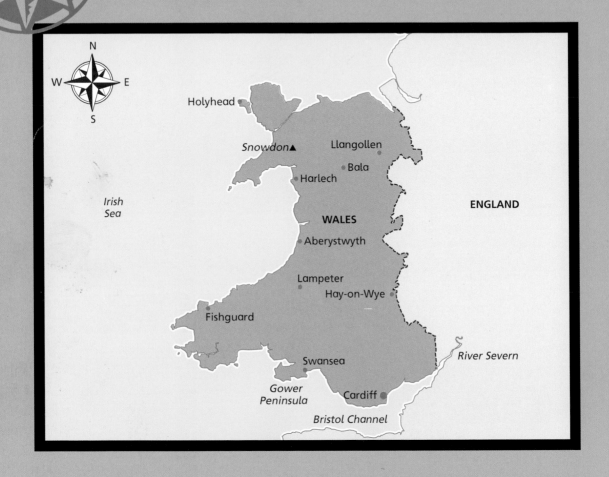

Wales is a country in the United
Kingdom. It is also part of a group of
islands called the British Isles. About
3 million people live in Wales.

The **capital** city of Wales is called Cardiff. This city is on the south **coast** of Wales. Cardiff has many old buildings, including this castle.

Land

South and mid Wales are green and hilly. The Gower **peninsula** in south Wales sticks out into the sea like a finger. It has wide, sandy beaches.

Many holiday-makers visit the
beaches of north Wales. **Inland**
from the **coast** are the mountains of
Snowdonia. The highest mountain is
Snowdon. It is 1085 metres high.

Landmarks

Wales has many beautiful castles. Most of them were built by the English king, Edward I. He ruled Wales over 700 years ago. This is Harlech Castle.

The Millennium **Stadium** in Cardiff is
the largest sports stadium in Wales.
Eighty thousand **spectators** can sit in
it. A sliding roof covers the pitch
when it rains.

Homes

Two-thirds of the people in Wales live in the cities of Cardiff and Swansea, in south Wales. Some live in smart flats like these, near the old **docks** in Cardiff.

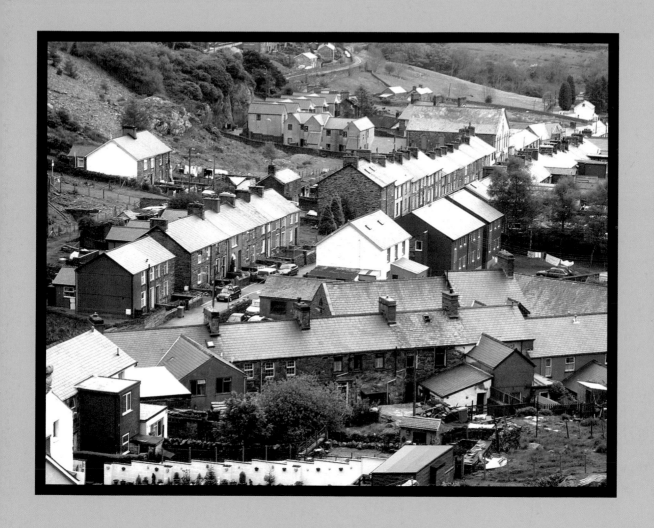

Many Welsh people used to work in coal and **slate** mines. Today, most of the mines are closed. **Terraced** houses like these were built as miners' homes.

Food

Laverbread is not bread at all. It is a type of seaweed found on the **coasts** of Wales. It is cooked in salty water and usually served on toast.

These are Welsh cheeses, cakes and breads. The loaf at the bottom is bara brith, which means 'speckled bread'. Welsh cakes, at the top, are a bit like scones.

Clothes

Young people in Wales wear casual clothes such as T-shirts, sweatshirts, jeans and training shoes. Clothes from top sports **designers** are very popular in Wales.

These women are wearing **traditional** Welsh **national costume**. Today, people in Wales only wear these costumes for special occasions, such as Welsh music and poetry festivals.

Work

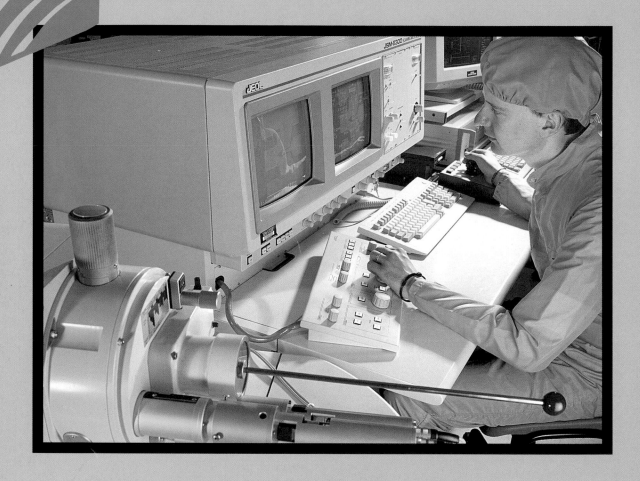

Two-thirds of Welsh people work in **service industries,** such as banks. Other people work in modern factories, making things like cars, televisions and computers.

More than three-quarters of the
countryside in Wales is farmland.
Farmers keep sheep and cattle in
the hills. Sheep dogs help them
round up and control the sheep.

Transport

The River Severn separates south Wales and England. It is very wide. Two huge bridges over the river let cars and lorries travel between the two countries.

This is Holyhead, a **port** on the island of Anglesey in north Wales. **Ferries** run from here to Ireland. Trains carry passengers from Holyhead to the rest of Wales and to England.

Language

Most Welsh people speak English.
About one person in every five
speaks Welsh as well. Welsh is
mainly spoken by people living
in north and west Wales.

In Wales, signs are written in Welsh and English so that everybody can understand them. The Welsh word for Wales, Cymru, is used in the top arrow.

School

In Wales, children go to **nursery school** when they are four years old. They start regular school when they are five years old. This class is in a city school in southern Wales.

This is a small school in a country town called Bala. Today, every school child in Wales learns to speak and write in Welsh, as well as English.

Free time

Welsh children play sports, such as rugby, football and netball. Rugby Union is very popular. It is the **national sport** of Wales.

People in Wales enjoy going to the seaside or **sightseeing** at the weekends and during school holidays. Wales has lots of beautiful countryside for walking or pony trekking.

Celebrations

St David is the **patron saint** of Wales. Welsh people wear the **traditional** symbols of the leek or the daffodil on St David's Day, 1 March.

Welsh festivals are called eisteddfods.
The International Eisteddfod is held in
Llangollen every July. Singers, dancers,
poets and musicians come from all
over the world to perform.

The Arts

Music is very popular in Wales. Many towns and villages have a **traditional** choir of men, called a male voice choir. They sing at concerts and local events.

The town of Hay-on-Wye in south-east Wales is famous for its bookshops. It has more than 25 shops selling second-hand books. A **literature** festival is held in Hay-on-Wye every summer.

Factfile

Name	Wales is the English name for the country. The Welsh call it Cymru.
Capital	The capital city of Wales is Cardiff.
Languages	Welsh people speak both English and Welsh.
Population	There are about 3 million people living in Wales.
Money	Welsh people use the British pound (£), which has 100 pence.
Religion	Many Welsh people are Christians, but there are also people of other religions, such as Muslims, Sikhs, Hindus, Jews and Buddhists.
Products	Wales has a lot of sheep farms, producing wool and meat. It produces a lot of iron and steel. Wales is a popular place for tourists to visit.

Welsh words you can learn

Cymru (say: CUmree)	Wales
bore da (say: boreh da)	good morning
hwyl fawr (say: hooil vowr)	goodbye
plis (say: plis)	please
prynhawn da (say: praown da)	good afternoon
Yr Wyddfa (say: ear withva)	Snowdon

Glossary

capital	most important city in a country
coast	edge of the land where it meets the sea
designer	person who plans what something will look like
docks	where ships are loaded and unloaded
ferries	passenger ships that go back and forth from one place to another
inland	land that is away from the sea
literature	to do with books, writers and writing
national costume	clothes that people used to wear in the past in a particular country
national sport	most important sport in a country
nursery school	place where young children begin learning
patron saint	saint who is said to look after a country
port	where ships arrive, carrying people and goods
peninsula	piece of land with sea on three sides
service industry	business that provides services for people to make their lives easier
sightseeing	visiting interesting or beautiful places
slate	grey stone, used mainly for making roof-tiles
spectators	people watching a sports game or event
stadium	place where many people watch sports or events
terraced	houses that are joined together in a line
traditional	something that has been done the same way for many years

Index

The y Draig Goch (Red Dragon) is the flag of wales.